Sandra Day O'Connor

Paving the Way

Dona Herweck Rice

Reader Consultants

Brian Allman, M.A.
Classroom Teacher, West Virginia

Cheryl Norman Lane, M.A.Ed.
Classroom Teacher
Chino Valley Unified School District

iCivics Consultants

Emma Humphries, Ph.D.
Chief Education Officer

Taylor Davis, M.T.
Director of Curriculum and Content

Natacha Scott, MAT
Director of Educator Engagement

Publishing Credits

Rachelle Cracchiolo, M.S.Ed., *Publisher*
Emily R. Smith, M.A.Ed., *VP of Content Development*
Véronique Bos, *Creative Director*
Dani Neiley, *Associate Content Specialist*
Fabiola Sepulveda, *Series Designer*
Cathrin Peterslund, *Illustrator, pages 6–9*

Image Credits: cover Getty Images/Wally McNamee; p4 Getty Images/Bettmann; p5 Newscom/Kevin Lamarque/Reuters; p10 Getty Images/Bettmann; p12 photo courtesy of Miguel Martinez; p13 Library of Congress [LC-DIG-highsm-53542]; p14 Library of Congress [LC-USZ62-60141]; p15, p17 Getty Images/Bettmann; p16 Associated Press; p18, p21 © The Republic-USA TODAY NETWORK; p22 Newscom/CNP/Michael Evans - White House; p23 Newscom/Arnie Sachs/picture alliance/Consolidated News Photos; p25 Newscom/CNP/Mark Wilson/Pool/Sipa USA; p27 photo courtesy of iCivics; p28 Alamy/World History Archive; p29 Newscom/Jason Reed/Reuters; all other images from iStock and/or Shutterstock

Library of Congress Cataloging-in-Publication Data

Names: Rice, Dona, author. | iCivics (Organization), other.
Title: Sandra Day O'Connor : paving the way / Dona Herweck Rice.
Description: Huntington Beach, CA : Teacher Created Materials, [2022] | "iCivics"--Cover. | Audience: Grades 4-6 | Summary: "Sandra Day O'Connor proved there are no limits to what one can accomplish. She did what no woman had ever before done-become a justice on the Supreme Court of the United States. O'Connor paved the way for women everywhere. She showed that women can become government leaders or achieve anything they want in life"-- Provided by publisher.
Identifiers: LCCN 2021054707 (print) | LCCN 2021054708 (ebook) | ISBN 9781087615493 (paperback) | ISBN 9781087630601 (ebook)
Subjects: LCSH: O'Connor, Sandra Day, 1930---Juvenile literature. | Women judges--United States--Biography--Juvenile literature. | United States. Supreme Court--Biography--Juvenile literature.
Classification: LCC KF8745.O25 R53 2022 (print) | LCC KF8745.O25 (ebook) | DDC 347.73/2634 [B]--dc23/eng/20211109
LC record available at https://lccn.loc.gov/2021054707
LC ebook record available at https://lccn.loc.gov/2021054708

TCM Teacher Created Materials
5482 Argosy Avenue
Huntington Beach, CA 92649
www.tcmpub.com

ISBN 978-1-0876-1549-3

Table of Contents

A New Day Dawns

It was not predestined that Sandra Day O'Connor would do great things. As a girl born in 1930, most professional options were closed to her from the beginning. But the Day family was filled with determination and **grit**. They were resilient, bright, and hardworking. So, too, was their little girl.

Sandra Day (right) and her mother, brother, and sister in 1940

These characteristics took Sandra Day from a cattle ranch in Arizona to one of the most **prestigious** law schools in the country. They took her from that law school to a seat in her state senate. They took her from the senate to a judgeship. And they took her from the judgeship to the Supreme Court of the United States.

This path of achievements was never before met by any woman in history. She paved the way for others to come. In fact, the "business as usual" way of the courts was flipped on its head the moment she became a Supreme Court justice. You might even say that a bright new day dawned for all.

Jump into Fiction

Carving a Way

The horse lowered its brown muzzle to the gray-green water. The girl at its side held the reins while she looked up across the expanse. Cottonwood and willow trees lined the running water. Upriver, a stony pink-colored canyon wall rose up to the cloud-tinted sky. The girl sighed deeply. She loved this river, and she loved this land.

The girl knew that the Gila River stretched from the mighty Colorado River that had chiseled out the Grand Canyon, drip by drip, over millions of years. She wondered if time and the water might do the same thing here, where the canyon walls already rose up tall and strong. "I guess these canyons are carved by the river, too, aren't they?" she thought aloud, the horse at her side. Then she laughed. Of course they were.

Patting her horse's neck and sure he'd drunk his fill, the girl climbed back into the saddle and tugged the reins to the left. The horse turned in that direction and started making its way next to the shore.

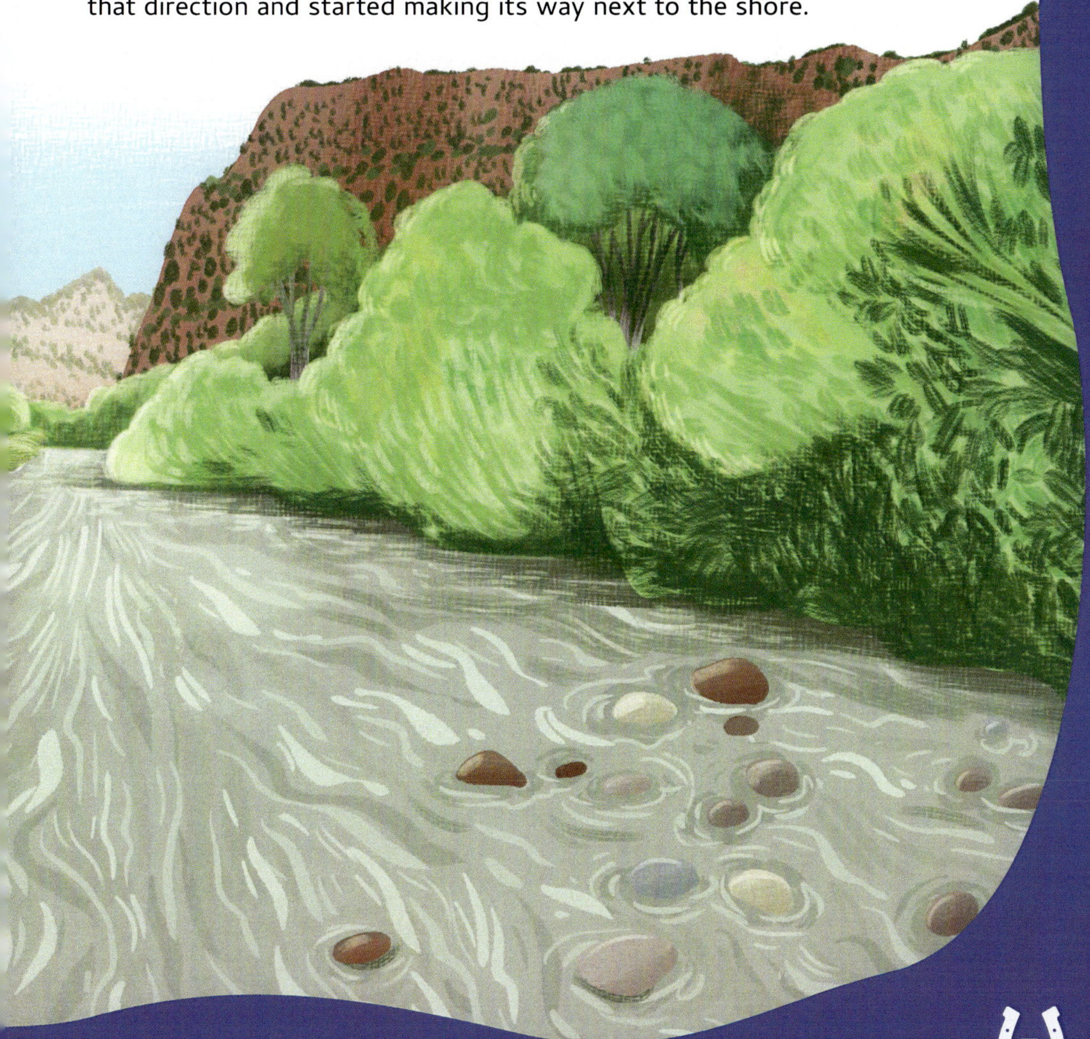

This land—these canyons, this river—were all the girl had ever known. She had always lived here. She felt that the land was a part of her now, and she was a part of the land.

She sat upright in her saddle, swaying rhythmically with the horse's steady trot. She breathed in deeply, filling her lungs. The scenery around her was magnificent, the river was persistent, and the horse below her was powerful. She felt inspired by them all, and they sparked an idea within her.

"If the land can be carved and changed," she wondered, "why can't I be?" She understood that she was shaped by the world around her—her parents, her siblings, and the life she led. But just maybe, she could use those things to carve something a little bigger, a little more meaningful, a little more than the person the world suggested she should be. Perhaps, instead, she could be whoever she chose to be.

The girl smiled, clicked her tongue, and clapped her boots to the horse's flanks. He sprang into a gallop, and the two rode breathless and free through the canyon and into the shining sun.

Back to Nonfiction

Getting Started

It was spring in El Paso, Texas, when Sandra Day was born. Harry and Ada Mae Day were proud parents as they welcomed their baby girl to the world. The day was March 26, 1930, and Sandra was the first of the Day children. Ann would arrive eight years later, and Alan would follow the year after that.

Sandra on her family's ranch

Think and Talk

How is your experience growing up like Sandra Day's? How is it different?

The Day children grew up on the Lazy B Ranch near Duncan, Arizona. It was a sprawling cattle ranch. The family home was about nine miles (14.5 kilometers) from the nearest paved road. There was no running water or electricity on the ranch when Day was born. These utilities were added to her home about the same time as her brother and sister.

When she was young, Day learned to hunt and fish. She even shot jackrabbits for the family meals when she was a little girl! The family valued being **self-sufficient** and resourceful. They believed that if there was a way for a person to be active and contribute to the family's well-being, then that is what they should do.

On the Move

Day learned to drive as soon as she was tall enough to reach the pedals and see over the dashboard. As a teenager, she could change a flat tire.

Because Day's family lived so far from a town, getting Day to school every day was a challenge. Her parents arranged for her to live with her grandmother in El Paso and go to school there. She attended the Radford School for Girls, a private school. She came home only for the summers and some holidays. Otherwise, she lived away from her parents and young brother and sister.

Radford School for Girls

During eighth grade, Day returned home for one year. She took a long bus ride every day to get to a school in the nearest town. Despite the long travel, she did well in school and was always a top student. In fact, she graduated high school with the sixth highest grade point average. Perhaps even more impressive, she was just sixteen years old when she did!

Despite her school commitments, Day was an active worker on the ranch when she was there. Hard work and dedication were expected of a Day. And Sandra Day always **delivered**.

By the Book

In her later years, Day wrote a book with her brother about their early life. It is called *Lazy B: Growing Up on a Cattle Ranch in the American Southwest.*

Becoming an Adult

Day was bright and eager, and she was college-bound. She was accepted to Stanford University in California. At just sixteen, she left home for college. She performed very well there and was the senior class president. Day graduated with honors in 1950. She continued at Stanford, earning her law degree in 1952. She placed third in her class!

While at Stanford, Day met and became friends with William Rehnquist. Like Day, Rehnquist was a bright, hardworking student and future judge. He had been a soldier during World War II and was in college on the GI Bill. The two friends shared notes and studied together. They dated for a while as well. After breaking up, the two continued their friendship—and their study partnership. When Rehnquist graduated, he wrote her a letter and proposed marriage. Day **declined** but they remained friends and always had great respect for each other.

Rehnquist was meant for a very bright future. He would go on to become the chief justice of the United States Supreme Court. He would play a role in Day's **nomination** there as well.

William H. Rehnquist

GI Bill

This government-funded program provides college and training money for people who have served in the U.S. armed forces. It was started in 1944. Many World War II veterans took advantage of it to jump-start their careers after returning home from the war.

Professional Life

Day did very well in school. But finding work was hard. Law firms did not want to hire a woman. She was offered a job as a legal secretary––a job far below her skills and training. She finally took a job without pay with the San Mateo County **district attorney**. She agreed to no pay so that she could get her foot in the door. She was not given an office; she had to share space with a secretary.

These pictures show Day during her years at Stanford.

But it did not take long for her employer to see her value. Day was made deputy district attorney in 1952. At the end of that same year, she also married John Jay O'Connor and added his name to hers. He was a year behind her in law school. When he graduated, he took a job as an attorney in Frankfurt, Germany. Day O'Connor went to Germany with her new husband. There, she became a **civilian** attorney for the U.S. Army.

The O'Connors returned to the United States in 1957. They moved to Phoenix, Arizona. Day O'Connor opened a **private practice** with a partner. She also did volunteer work in her community. And she began to raise her growing family.

Motherhood

The O'Connors had three sons. Their first, Scott, was born in 1957. Brian followed in 1960. Jay, the third, arrived in 1962.

Judge to Justice

Day O'Connor did well in her private practice. But she felt a call to return to **public service**. It was a call she would answer for the rest of her career.

In 1965, she became the Arizona assistant attorney general. Day O'Connor was a rising star in Arizona. She was known for her intelligence, service, and hard work. In 1969, a position in the Arizona state senate became open. Governor Jack Williams appointed her to the job. She then won reelection twice. And, she was nominated by her senate **peers** as **majority leader**. Many other members had more senior roles than she did. She was not the likely choice for this role. But no one could deny her talent and ability. Day O'Connor became the first woman in the United States to hold this position.

Day O'Connor taking the oath of office at the Arizona Capitol in 1969

As a state senator, Day O'Connor worked for the people of her state. She had respect for the **political** system. The law mattered. She cared about having **civil discourse** with her peers. Members of the senate have many different ideas. But their job is to work together for the good of the people. Day O'Connor worked to make this happen.

Arizona State Capitol

Majority Leader

The majority leader belongs to the party with the most members in the Senate. This person takes the lead in deciding which issues will be discussed there. They lead debates on those issues as well. Other senators look to them to guide the work they do.

A Move to the Judicial Branch

Day O'Connor could have continued in the state **legislature** for many years. She was successful there. But she chose to make a change in 1974. This is when she left the Senate and entered the **judicial branch** of government. She was elected as a superior court judge.

People thought of her as fair but firm. They trusted her to do her job well. In 1979, she was appointed to serve on the Arizona Court of Appeals.

Outside the courtroom at this time, Day O'Connor's interest in politics grew as well. She believed in **civic engagement**. She thought all people should be involved in the world around them. And she always strived to do her part.

Day O'Connor also believed in the good that women could do when they were an active part of civic processes. To this end, she helped found the Arizona Women Lawyers Association. She also founded the National Association of Women Judges. Few women of her time were lawyers and judges, so she did what she could to help change things for the future.

Day O'Connor receives her robe for the Court of Appeals.

Appeals

When decisions are made in court, they can be appealed. This means the decision is reviewed in another court. The court of appeals—or *appellate* court—might change the ruling.

The U.S. Supreme Court

In 1981, Ronald Reagan was president of the United States. One of the president's jobs is to fill openings on the U.S. Supreme Court. This is the top court in the country. Judges on the court—called *justices*—are nominated by the president. The U.S. Senate approves the appointment. New justices are able to serve on the court for the rest of their lives. They may also choose to retire.

At this time, only men had served as justices. But President Reagan had made a promise when elected. He said he would nominate a woman to the court if he had the chance. When Justice Potter Stewart retired, Reagan had that chance.

Sandra Day O'Connor is sworn in as the first female justice on the U.S. Supreme Court.

Reagan spoke with a justice on the Supreme Court. This was William Rehnquist, Day O'Connor's old friend. Rehnquist suggested to Reagan that he should consider Day O'Connor. Reagan did just that.

Day O'Connor's abilities were undeniable. She was a great choice. Reagan nominated her in July. The U.S. Senate **confirmed** her by unanimous vote. On September 25, 1981, Day O'Connor became the first female justice in the 191-year history of the court.

A Big Decision

"His decision was as much a surprise to me as it was to the nation as a whole. But Ronald Reagan knew that his decision wasn't about Sandra Day O'Connor. It was about women everywhere. It was about a nation that was on its way to bridging a **chasm** between genders that had divided us for too long."

—Sandra Day O'Connor

Day O'Connor made her mark on the court right away. She proved from the beginning that she was a free thinker. She became a leader who was known for her wealth of knowledge and common sense.

Often, Day O'Connor cast a deciding vote on the court. She was a **moderate**. She did not have extreme views in any direction. She weighed her decisions carefully and decided for herself.

While serving on the court, Day O'Connor also had a major health challenge. In 1988, she was diagnosed with breast cancer. She quietly received treatment and recovered. She did not reveal her cancer battle publicly until years later.

She remained the only woman on the court until Ruth Bader Ginsburg was appointed in 1993. Three more women have since been appointed, one replacing Bader Ginsburg after she died.

Day O'Connor served on the court for 24 years. In time, her husband became quite ill. She cared for him for a long time and remained on the court. Ultimately, she chose to retire in 2006.

There is no question that Sandra Day O'Connor left a valuable legacy on the U.S. Supreme Court. And she changed the face of the court forever.

Think and Talk

What lasting impact did Sandra Day O'Connor have on the world?

Supreme Court Justices in 2003

And Then There Were Nine

When the U.S. Supreme Court began, it did not have nine justices as it does now. At first, there were six and then seven. Later, the number grew to nine and then ten. In 1869, Congress decided on nine. It has stayed that way ever since, although Congress could change the number again.

Legacy

Day O'Connor was known for more than just her work on the Supreme Court. She was also an author who wrote several books. She wrote a children's book called *Finding Susie*. She wrote another children's book called *Chico*. It was published not long before she retired. Near the end of her time on the Supreme Court, she also wrote a book about her time on the court. A while later, she wrote one more about the history of the Supreme Court.

Day O'Connor also became an active speaker. She gave speeches for eager audiences around the world. People wanted to know about her life and thoughts.

The year she retired, Day O'Connor put her passion for civics to work. She started an online organization. Its purpose is to help students build their civic knowledge. She called it *iCivics*. Day O'Connor said, "We have a complex system of government. You have to teach it to every generation." The goal of iCivics is to do just that.

She founded the Sandra Day O'Connor Institute in 2009. Its goal is to "advance civil discourse, civic engagement, and civics education" for all people.

Women in Law

When Day O'Connor graduated from law school, two percent of law students were women. When she retired, that number had jumped to 48 percent. In 2006, Arizona State University renamed its law school for Sandra Day O'Connor.

In her later years, Sandra Day O'Connor made an impact on civics education.

After her many years of service, Day O'Connor was honored with a special award. President Barack Obama gave her the Presidential Medal of Freedom. It is the highest honor offered to a civilian.

Obama had glowing things to say. He talked about the people receiving the medal: "They have made their mark in the courtroom, in the community, and in Congress." He added "our lives are what we make of them, and the truest test of a person's life is what we do for one another." Day O'Connor passed this test with flying colors.

1999 portrait by Danni Dawson

President Barack Obama honors Day O'Connor with the Presidential Medal of Freedom in 2009.

She stayed active in public life until 2018. Health challenges then forced her to withdraw into a more private life. But her presence throughout the country remains in the work she has done. It remains in the service she gave, too. Sandra Day O'Connor paved a way for others. She carved a bright path that any eager, driven, and civic-minded person might follow.

Glossary

chasm—a major division, separation, or difference between two people or groups

civic engagement—individual or group activities that help to make a difference in communities

civil discourse—polite conversation about community concerns and government

civilian—a person who is not part of the police or military

confirmed—approved

declined—said no

delivered—did or said what a person said they would

district attorney—a lawyer responsible for starting legal cases against people accused of crimes in a community

grit—courage; strength of character in hardship

judicial branch—the part of the government that includes the court system

legislature—a group of people who make or change laws

majority leader—the chosen head of a group that has the most members overall, especially in politics

moderate—a person whose political ideas are not extreme

nomination—the act of formally choosing someone as a candidate for a job

peers—people who belong to the same group, such as age or experience

political—having to do with government and how it is run

prestigious—worthy of respect and admiration

private practice—a professional business that is owned by an individual and not owned or paid for by the government or a larger company

public service—work that someone does as part of a government

self-sufficient—able to live or function without help

Index

Civics in Action

A hero is a special person. A hero uses their strengths to do good for their community. Sandra Day O'Connor is an American hero. There are many other heroes today and in the past. They are not always given the recognition they deserve. You can help people learn about these heroes!

1. Research an American hero of your choice.
2. Create a display about your hero. You could create a poster, a brochure, or another type of display.
3. Share your display with other students in your school.
4. Celebrate all the American heroes!